Formal Meetings

Formal Meetings

How to Preside
and Participate

Alice N. Pohl

NTC Business Books
a division of *NTC Publishing Group* • Lincolnwood, Illinois USA

About the Author

From her many years of experience as teacher and consultant, Alice N. Pohl has acquired a practical insight into the questions and problems confronting all types of organizations regarding parliamentary procedure.

Pohl is the Accrediting Director for the American Institute of Parliamentarians. She is the author of several books and a variety of articles on parliamentary procedure.

Published by NTC Business Books, a division of NTC Publishing Group.
© 1990 by NTC Publishing Group, 4255 West Touhy Avenue,
Lincolnwood (Chicago), Illinois 60646-1975 U.S.A.
Manufactured in the United States of America.
Library of Congress Catalog Card Number: 89-63136

0 ML 9 8 7 6 5 4 3 2 1

Contents

Chapter 1

Meetings and Sessions

A *meeting* is a single gathering of an organization's members in one area to transact business. A *session* is a meeting or series of meetings devoted to a single order of business, a program, an agenda, or any other announced purpose; when there is more than one meeting, each succeeding meeting continues the business at the point where it was left off. *Formal Meetings: How to Preside & Participate* is designed to help readers use parliamentary procedure to most effectively participate in meetings and sessions, both as officers and as members of an organization.

The Basics of Parliamentary Procedure

Every decision-making body has some rules that it has adopted. These rules apply whenever the group makes a decision. If the group fails to conform to them, the decision becomes invalid. Similarly, every member of a group is presumed to be equal and to have rights that must be protected. If members do not make appropriate use of their rights, however, they may lose them.

Parliamentary procedure is a set of formalized rules for decision-making groups. The rules have been developed to expedite business and to help organizations carry out their aims. Parliamentary procedure makes it easier for the members of an organization to work together harmoniously and to protect the rights of the majority, the minority, and the absentee.

The principles of parliamentary procedure are simple and logical. They include the following:

1. The organization must meet to make a decision. Proper notice of the meeting, including the time, place, and purpose, must be given to all members of the organization.

2. There must be a quorum present at the meeting.

3. The decision that the organization makes must be based on some question. The question may be written or spoken. Members have the right to know what the question is and what its effects will be before they vote on it.

4. There must be opportunity to debate the question. It is a member's right to hear and to be heard.

5. The question must be decided by taking a vote. With a few exceptions, the majority position in the vote becomes the decision of the organization. No member can be compelled to vote; however, anyone who does not vote has the effect of voting with the prevailing side.

6. Any decision reached is considered null and void if it is in conflict with any higher authority, such as the

constitution, bylaws, or other rules of the organization, or any national, state, or local law.

7. The decision belongs to the majority, but the rights to discuss, to be heard, and to oppose are valued rights of the minority. These rights must be protected.

8. If a subject has been voted on, it may not be presented again in the same form. The only way to bring a subject back for consideration at the same meeting is to move to reconsider the vote taken on the subject.

These eight rules are the most basic components of parliamentary procedure. Everything else builds on these components to ensure that the goals and rights of a group are met. *Formal Meetings: How to Preside & Participate* is dedicated to showing you how parliamentary procedure fits together, so that you can use it confidently and effectively in formal meeting situations, whether you are the presiding officer, the secretary, or one of the other members.

Conducting a Meeting

The officers required to conduct a meeting are the presiding officer and the secretary. The minimum number of persons who must be present at a meeting for a business to be legally transacted is the quorum of the membership. The quorum refers to the number present, and not to the number actually voting on a particular question.

Meetings may include three parts: the opening, which may include a prayer (if appropriate), pledge to the flag, song, welcome, or introductions; the business; and the closing, which may include a program or speaker. The business portion of the meeting includes the agenda—all the subjects that must be attended to, and the order in which they are to be considered.

Order of Business

The essential parts of a business meeting are (1) call to order; (2) minutes; (3) reports of officers, boards, and committees; (4) unfinished business; (5) new business; and (6) adjournment. Table 1.1 shows a typical order of business. The regular order of business should be followed, allowing for reasonable flexibility. There is no standard rule for including other topics in the order of business. Each organization decides where it inserts these items.

Table 1.1

Typical Order of Business

Reading and approval of minutes

Reports of officers

Reports of boards (cabinet, council, executive committee)

Reports of standing committees

Reports of special committees

Special orders (orders that were not disposed of at the previous meeting)

Unfinished business (general orders)

New business

Some organizations include "good of the order" or "organization welfare" after new business. This allows for specific suggestions, constructive comments, criticism, or compliments. No motions may be proposed during this time.

The order of business for a special meeting consists only of the call to order, consideration of the items stated in the notice of the meeting, and adjournment.

Sample Agenda

The agenda of a meeting governs the business that must be attended to during that meeting. The items included in a typical agenda are covered below. Any item of business on the agenda can be taken out of order by adopting a motion to suspend the rules. This motion requires a two-thirds vote or general consent.

Call to Order.   The presiding officer calls the meeting to order promptly at the scheduled time with one tap of the gavel. The secretary then ascertains whether or not a quorum is present. If a quorum is not present, business cannot be legally conducted at the meeting.

Reading and Approval of Minutes.   The first business in order is reading and approving the minutes of the previous meeting. After corrections have been made, the minutes are approved as corrected. Corrections may be approved by general consent. If the organization has a committee to correct and approve the minutes, the chair announces the fact.

Reports of Officers.   At an annual meeting, the officers report in the order in which they are listed in the bylaws of the organization. At regular meetings, the presiding officer usually calls on the treasurer to report first. The treasurer reports the income and expenses since the previous meeting. The presiding officer then asks if there are any questions. After the treasurer answers the questions, the presiding officer states that the report will be placed on file. No vote is taken on the treasurer's report.

Reports of Committees.   The report of the board of directors or governing body is given first. A summary of the action taken by the board may be given. If the board presents a recommendation, it is considered and voted upon at this time. No second from the assembly is required.

Only those standing committees with a report to give should be called upon. Written reports are worded in the third person ("the committee determined"). No action is taken on an informational report.

If there is a nominating committee, it makes its report after the other standing committees. No vote is taken on the nominating committee's report.

Special committees that are to report are called on in the order in which they were appointed.

Special Orders.   Items of business that have been made special orders are taken in the order in which they were made. A *special order* is an item of business that must be considered at a certain time because the assembly has voted to consider it then.

General Orders and Unfinished Business.   A *general order* is any question that, usually by postponement, has been made an order of the day without being made a special order. *Unfinished business* is a question that was pending when the previous meeting adjourned, a question that was unfinished at the previous meeting, or a matter that was postponed. The chair should not ask for unfinished business. He or she should have a list of all subjects.

An item that was laid on the table (in order to attend to more pressing business) may be taken from the table at this time or under new business.

New Business. Correspondence which requires action should be brought up at this time. Items laid on the table also may be brought up, since they are not automatically on the agenda. Additionally, members may introduce new items of business.

Announcements. The chair may make, or call upon another member to make, any necessary announcements. After the announcements, the chair may adjourn the meeting. No motion is necessary.

Quorum

Since it is seldom possible to have every member present at each meeting, it is necessary to allow a certain proportion of the membership, the *quorum*, to transact the business of the organization. If a majority of the membership is present, business can be transacted, regardless of the number of members actually voting.

The number that constitutes a quorum is usually stated in the constitution or bylaws of the organization. The quorum should be based on the number of members that can be depended on to be present at any meeting. If there is no provision for what constitutes a quorum, the quorum is a majority of the total membership of the organization. The requirement of a quorum is a protection against unrepresentative action by a small number of persons. It is a legal and common practice to fix the quorum at less than a majority of the membership. If the provision for a quorum is a small proportion of the total membership, rigid requirements for notices of meetings should be established, so that all members will have an opportunity to be present.

When there is no provision for a quorum in the bylaws, common parliamentary law determines the quorum as follows:

1. In a mass meeting, the quorum is those present.

2. In ordinary organizations whose bylaws do not specify a quorum, the quorum is a majority of all members.

3. In a conference or convention in which there are delegates, unless provided otherwise, the quorum is a majority of qualified delegates who have been registered as attending, whether or not some have left.

4. In organizations in which there are no required dues, and for which the membership list may not be reliable, the quorum is those attending the meeting.

5. In committees or boards, the quorum is a majority of the members of the committee or board. A committee or board does not have the power to determine its quorum, unless the bylaws authorize it.

Proceedings in the Absence of a Quorum

If the organization's rules require that a meeting be held, the absence of a quorum does not prevent calling the meeting to order. The minutes must show that the rules were complied with and the meeting held.

The only actions that can be legally transacted in the absence of a quorum are the following:

- To fix the time of adjournment
- To adjourn
- To take a recess in order to try to obtain a quorum

Regular business cannot be transacted in the absence of a quorum. However, emergency action can be taken and confirmed or approved at the next meeting. The motion to *ratify* (approve or confirm) is used to validate an action already taken without a quorum present.

While business cannot legally be transacted in the absence of a quorum, a quorum is not required for certain actions. Committee reports can be received for information (but no action may be taken on them). The program of the day also can be given.

When a member notices the absence of a quorum, he or she can make a point of order to that effect at any time, as long as the point of order does not interrupt the person speaking. When the chair notices the absence of a quorum, he or she can entertain a motion to adjourn or to take a recess to contact members and ask 'hem to attend. In organizations that have the power to ' ompel members to attend, a "call of the house" can be ordered.

The quorum for all meetings should be established in a section of the bylaws. An amendment to the bylaws goes into effect immediately upon its adoption. The proper procedure to amend that part of the bylaws is to strike out the old provision or number and insert the new provision. This should be made and voted upon as one motion. If the number is simply struck, the quorum instantly becomes a majority of the membership.

Motions

A *motion* is a formal statement of a proposal for consideration by the assembly. The essential steps by which a motion is brought before the assembly are listed below:

1. A member rises, addresses the chair, then waits for recognition.

2. The chair recognizes the member.

3. The member proposes the motion by saying, "I move that . . . ."

4. Another member seconds the motion without rising or addressing the chair. A second implies the seconder wishes the motion to be considered by the assembly. It does not indicate that the seconder favors the motion; he or she may wish to speak against it or vote against it. If a motion is not seconded, it is not considered before the assembly. The chair proceeds to the next item of business.

5. The chair states the motion, which then becomes the question: "It is moved and seconded that . . . . Is there any discussion?" If the wording is not clear, the chair should put it into suitable form. The motion should be recorded in the minutes as the chair has stated it.

6. During discussion, speakers must: be entitled to the floor; address their remarks to the chair, be courteous, and avoid speaking about personalities; confine the discussion to the pending question; observe the rules as to the number of times and length of time a speaker may speak to a question; ask for information; this is not counted as debate.

7. The chair puts the question by saying, "Those in favor of the motion that . . . say Aye. Those opposed,

say No." The chair always must call for the negative vote and tell the assembly what to say. If the voice vote is in doubt, a rising vote or show of hands may be taken.

8. The chair must announce the result of the vote. If the vote is tied, the motion is lost. The chair may vote to make or break a tie vote.

Assumed Motions

Because the presiding officer is responsible for expediting business, the chair may *assume the motion*, that is, state the question without waiting for a formal motion by a member.

For example, after the reading of the minutes, the chair may simply state, "The minutes are approved as read." If a committee presents a special report, the chair may say, "The question is on the adoption of the committee's recommendation. Is there any discussion?"

General Consent

In routine business or matters of little importance, where there seems to be no objection, time often can be saved by using *general consent* (also called *unanimous consent*).

To obtain general consent, the chair states, "If there is no objection" or "Is there any objection to . . . ?" The chair then pauses and continues, "Hearing no objection, we will . . . ." If anyone does call out "Objection," the chair formally states the question and takes a vote to determine the result.

General consent does not imply that every member is in favor of the proposed action; it means that the opposition may feel it is useless to oppose or discuss the matter.

For example, if a speaker's time in debate has expired and he or she asks for additional time, the chair may say, "If there is no objection, the member's time will be extended."

Amendments to motions are sometimes so simple or acceptable that they may be adopted by general consent. The chair may say, "If there is no objection, the words . . . will be inserted; the wording of the motion then will be . . . ."

Chapter 2

The Presiding Officer

The most important officer in a decision-making organization is the presiding officer. The exact title of the presiding officer is usually designated in the bylaws of the organization. That person may be designated "president," "chair," "chief," "moderator," or "executive officer."

The word *president* comes from the Latin word *praesidere*, which means "one who presides or is in charge of a meeting." By custom, the president never refers to him- or herself as "I" while presiding. Instead, the president uses the word chair—meaning the seat of office or authority—as in, "The chair recognizes Ms. West."

Presiding is an art. It is a combination of tact, understanding, and awareness. The president should be able to draw out ideas from the members of the group, to make them feel free and comfortable in participating in the discussion. However, the president also should be able to maintain control of the meeting and to keep it focused. A major cause of confusion in any meeting is a president who fails to keep members informed about pending business.

Although a president's specific role and responsibilities usually are stated in the bylaws of the organization, some responsibilities are common to all group leaders.

First, presidents must train themselves to speak up. A presiding officer should make sure that those sitting in the rear of the room are able to hear what is going on. Conversely, presiding officers must train themselves to be good listeners. Presidents should always remain neutral, listening to the voice of the minority and obeying the will of the majority.

Second, presidents must be able to exercise good judgment, common sense, and tact. They should be impartial, courteous, and fair—regardless of how other participants are behaving. Presiding officers should keep in mind that they have been elected or appointed to guide the affairs of the organization. A president is not chosen to be a passive observer—but she or he is not chosen to be a dictator, either.

Third, presidents should be well-versed in the organization's bylaws and standing rules. Presiding officers should always be prepared to answer any questions that may arise concerning the organization. They also should be prepared to retain what is good and discard what is bad about past practices. Tradition for tradition's sake is not always wise.

Finally, presiding officers must have precise knowledge of parliamentary procedure. They must be able to keep meetings moving effectively and to insure equality of opportunity in decision-making.

Duties of the President

In addition to the general responsibilities outlined above, a president has specific duties during a meeting. The duties include preparing for the meeting, calling the meeting to order, chairing the meeting, and knowing when and how to conclude it.

Preparation

One of the best ways to prepare for a major meeting is to hold a preliminary meeting. The preliminary meeting may consist of other officers and committee chairs. The purpose of the preliminary meeting is to present goals or to see that goals are set for the major meeting.

At the preliminary meeting, the *agenda* for the major meeting can be set. The agenda is the plan for the meeting, the order in which issues will be handled. The presiding officer should check with committee chairs to see if they are ready to report and to let them know the order in which they will be called upon. The presiding officer also should check with the secretary to see if there is any unfinished business from the previous meeting. The order for addressing unfinished business should be established first, then new business should be added to the agenda.

Finally, the presiding officer should assemble the materials he or she will need at the meeting. These include copies of the organization's bylaws and standing rules and a list of the standing committee chairs. If the presiding officer is not familiar with the precedence of motions, a chart of motions should be on hand. If there is a parliamentarian present at meetings, the president should consult with that person to make sure that the business is in order.

A president should always be ready well before a meeting. However, emergencies do happen. The most carefully planned agenda may have to be altered at the last minute to allow for more pressing business. Presiding officers must be flexible and honest, and keep the members informed.

Calling the Meeting to Order

The presiding officer should call the meeting to order at the appointed time. If a president is consistently late, the members will begin to come late, and schedules will continue to slide further and further back. The president should make sure that a quorum is present before beginning the meeting. The gavel may be used to call the meeting to order.

Chairing the Meeting

The presiding officer announces the business that should come before the assembly in the proper order. He or she should keep things moving. This includes recognizing members at the appropriate times and making sure they address the chair before they begin to speak. Members who attempt to speak before they are recognized by the chair should be called to order. The president also is responsible for making sure that speakers conclude their comments within designated time limits.

The president is responsible for making sure that all members understand the pending business. All motions that have been properly proposed (offered in the correct form and seconded) should be clearly stated—and repeated if necessary. If a motion is too long or complicated, the president should ask to have it submitted in writing. If members are confused about a motion, the president should impartially explain its effects.

The presiding officer does not participate in debate. If the presiding officer wishes to participate, he or she must relinquish the chair to a vice-president who is present, or to a ranking vice-president who has not spoken on the motion. If no vice-president is in the room, or if the vice-president declines to take the chair on the grounds of wishing to speak to the motion, the president must designate another member to take the chair. That person must be approved by the assembly.

One of the presiding officer's most difficult duties is restricting discussion to the question before the group. The president must be tactful in stopping discussion that does not relate to the matter at hand. One technique is to alternate between members speaking in favor of the motion and those speaking in opposition to it. If a member's position on the question is uncertain, the president should ask which side that person will speak on. Another technique for focusing the debate is to politely interrupt the speaker, repeat the motion, and state that the comments are not germane to the subject.

Another of the president's duties is to answer parliamentary inquiries and questions. She or he should decide questions of order and rule improper motions out of order. The president should be courteous when giving rulings on points of order or questions of procedure.

After a motion has been discussed, the presiding officer is responsible for putting it to a vote. The question is stated exactly, and then the vote is taken. The president should call for the negative vote, even if the vote seems to be all in the affirmative. The results of each vote should be announced clearly.

Adjourning the Meeting

The president can adjourn the meeting. No motion is necessary. However, the president should remind the members of the unfinished business before actually adjourning the meeting.

Procedure and the President

A certain number of parliamentary procedures affect only the presiding officer. The procedures are designed to ensure that the president will run meetings efficiently and democratically.

Parliamentary Motions Concerning the President

The president relinquishes the chair when he or she wishes to participate in the debate. There are a few exceptions to this rule. When the president is a candidate for reelection or has been nominated to be a delegate, he or she continues to preside.

However, if a motion is made requesting the resignation of the president, the chair should be relinquished to the vice-president. Similarly, if a motion is made that refers to the president in a capacity not shared with other members, he or she should relinquish the chair.

Voting Rights of the President

So that the presiding officer's vote does not unduly influence the rest of the assembly, certain parliamentary procedures govern how the president may vote.

The president does not join in a voice vote. Similarly, in a standing or show-of-hands vote, the president does not participate in the first count.

On the other hand, the president does vote when the vote is taken by ballot. The president also participates in a roll-call vote, but he or she votes last.

The president may vote when the vote will affect the results, that is, when the president's vote will cause a tie and defeat the motion or will make or break the required two-thirds. However, the president is not obliged to cast the vote that will affect the result.

Other Rights of the President

Holding office does not deprive the president of the rights of a member. However, the impartiality required of the chair precludes exercising these rights while presiding. As noted above, the president has the right to vacate the chair in order to participate in a debate. On an appeal, the president has the right to remain in the chair. In these instances, the president may speak twice—first and last.

By virtue of the office, the president is an *ex-officio* member of committees only if designated in the bylaws. This means the president has the same rights as other committee members, but he or she is not required to attend committee meetings and is not counted when determining a quorum. The ex-officio authority cannot be delegated to the vice-president or another member.

Presidential Protocol

Parliamentary procedure calls for the presiding officer to follow certain protocol. The protocol dictates when the president stands, sits, and leaves the chair.

According to protocol, the president stands for the following:

- Calling the meeting to order
- Adjourning the meeting

- Stating the question

- Putting the question to the assembly

- Explaining reasons for rulings on points of order

- Speaking on a point of order or an appeal

The president is seated or steps back from the lectern or microphone when the floor is assigned to another member.

Since no action is usually taken, the president does not leave the chair to make his or her report. The exception to this rule is when the report contains a resolution. In this case, the president would leave the chair until the resolution has been decided by the members.

Parliamentary Phrases

The presiding officer must be well versed in parliamentary procedure. To ensure the confidence of the members, the presiding officer should be careful to word motions and business properly. Some of the most useful parliamentary phrases are listed here:

- The meeting will please come to order.

- The secretary will read the minutes of the _____ meeting.

- We will now hear the _____ report.

- Are there any questions concerning the _____ report?

- The first business in order is . . . .

- The next business in order is . . . .

- New business is now in order.

- The chair recognizes . . . .

- It is moved and seconded that . . . .
- It is moved and seconded to amend the motion by . . . .
- Hearing no second, the motion is not before you at this time.
- The motion is not in order at this time.
- Please repeat your motion.
- Those in favor of the motion . . . please say Aye.
- Those opposed to the motion, say No.
- The Ayes have it; the motion is carried.
- The Ayes have it; the amendment is carried. Is there further discussion on the motion as amended?
- If there is no objection, the chair will . . . .
- For what reason does the member rise?
- If there is no further business, the meeting is adjourned.

Restrictions on Presidential Power

Parliamentary procedure contains a number of restrictions on presidential power. These restrictions exist as a check on the presiding officer.

If the presiding officer will not be able to attend a meeting, he or she cannot authorize another member to preside. The substitute must be chosen by the members. Similarly, the presiding officer cannot conduct official business by phone—except by conference phone.

During a meeting, the president has a number of restrictions on his or her actions. The presiding officer cannot do the following:

- Ask a member to second a motion

- Close debate, so long as any member who has not exhausted his or her right to speak still desires the floor

- Vote twice—once as a member and again as presiding officer

- Depart from the prescribed order of business once the agenda has been adopted by the members

- Debate while in the chair, except on an appeal

- Take from the table a motion that was laid on the table

- Take sides

- Take a voice vote if the bylaws require a ballot vote

- Declare a vote unanimous unless the motion was voted on by ballot and there are no negative votes

- Impose a penalty or order an offending member from the meeting

The President-Elect

Some organizations elect a president one term in advance. In such a case, the members do not vote for a candidate for the office of president. Instead, they elect a *president-elect* and the other officers of the organization. The president-elect automatically becomes the president in the next term. This office exists only if provided for in the bylaws.

Once a person has been elected president-elect, the organization cannot alter the decision regarding the succession or vacate the office for other reasons.

The president-elect may assume the duties of the president when that officer is absent or incapacitated; however, this must be provided for in the bylaws. If this provision has not been made, the first vice-president presides and completes the president's term.

The Past President

A *past president* is one who has served to the end of a term or has died before the expiration of that term.

If the bylaws of an organization state that the *immediate* past president automatically becomes a member of the board, only the person who served as president at the end of that term may serve.

Ex-Officio

In some organizations, the bylaws provide that the president is an ex-officio member of all committees except the nominating committee. This gives the president the same rights as the other committee members; however, he or she is not required to attend the meetings and is not counted in determining a quorum.

In some organizations, the board includes other ex-officio members. These persons are members of the board because they hold a particular office or a committee chair. An ex-officio member has the same rights, responsibilities, and duties as other members, including the right to vote.

Chapter 3

The Secretary

Although there are many kinds of secretaries, the simple term *secretary* usually means the recording secretary. In some organizations, this officer is called the clerk or recorder. This chapter is concerned only with the recording secretary.

Secretaries handle a variety of details in addition to being in charge of the records, minutes of the meeting, and related affairs of the organization. The secretary is an official who sits close to the presiding officer and observes all the proceedings carefully. By taking notes, the secretary is able to explain at any time what business is pending. As a member of the organization, the secretary does not forfeit any rights of membership. He or she retains the right to make motions, enter into discussion, and vote.

The secretary should have an understanding of the purpose of the organization and the procedures used to accomplish its goals. The secretary also must keep legible minutes, letters, and other records. The ability to read aloud effectively is another valuable skill.

Duties of the Secretary

The duties of the secretary may include preparing the agenda, taking notes, and keeping the secretary's book. Secretaries also may have other duties.

Order of Business and Agenda

Matters to be brought up at a meeting usually are known in advance. By preparing a list of topics as an outline, the secretary can help avoid confusion and ensure that all important items are covered. An *order of business* should be given to the presiding officer to help prepare the agenda. The order of business includes the committees that are ready to report and the unfinished business from the last meeting.

An *agenda* is a list of the specific items under each order of business that the presiding officer will present to the membership. The secretary can prepare or assist the president in preparing the agenda. The agenda enables members to know in advance when each item of business will be considered.

Some organizations may have an established order of business in their rules. A recognized pattern for the order of business follows:

1. Reading and approval of minutes

2. Reports of officers, boards, and standing committees

3. Reports of special committees

4. Unfinished business

5. New business

6. Announcements

Each organization decides where it will insert other topics, such as roll call, payment of bills, correspondence, initiations, and inductions. If correspondence requires action by the assembly, it is read under new business and acted upon at that time.

Presiding

In the absence of the president or vice-president, the secretary calls the meeting to order and presides until a temporary chair, or a *chair pro tem*, is elected. The secretary should be familiar with the procedures for calling a meeting to order and presiding over the election of the chair pro tem.

Taking Notes

The secretary should have an outline of the items to be presented and copies of reports before the meeting begins. A list of the members should be on hand to check the names of those present or absent. The secretary should note those who arrive late and those who leave early, since an important issue may hinge on whether or not a certain member was present.

Secretaries should be sure to record the exact wording of motions. If a motion was not heard or understood, the secretary should interrupt the proceedings to get the exact wording. If business is left unfinished, secretaries should be sure to note the items that must be taken up at the next meeting.

The secretary should take notes that are accurate and thorough. These complete notes will help in writing the *minutes* that will be read at the next meeting. While notes are taken in depth, minutes are written in summary. It is always a good idea to transcribe the notes as soon as possible, while they are still fresh. It is also a good idea to hold on to the complete meeting notes until after the minutes have been approved.

The Secretary's Book

The secretary's book is the property of the organization. It should contain copies of the constitution, bylaws, standing rules, policies, procedures, current membership list, and committee lists. Copies of all minutes also should be included, in consecutive order. Written reports should be attached to the minutes or placed in a file. For ease of reference, it is helpful to keep meeting notes together and to number the pages to correspond with agenda items.

Other Duties

Secretaries may be responsible for a number of other duties. These duties may include sending out notice of meetings to the membership; providing paper for voting at meetings; furnishing committees with necessary documents; notifying officers, committee members, and delegates of their election or appointment; and following up on all action after the meeting.

Secretaries also may be responsible for conducting the correspondence of the organization. In some cases, a separate officer is elected or appointed to handle correspondence.

Another duty of the secretary is to make sure that the bylaws are correctly typed. The secretary should make necessary corrections in the numbering of articles, sections, or other subdivisions of the bylaws after they have been amended.

If a vote must be conducted by mail, the secretary should furnish the officials in charge of issuing the ballot with a list of the names and mailing addresses of all persons entitled to vote.

The Minutes

One of the most important responsibilities of the secretary is to prepare and present the minutes of each meeting. The minutes, prepared from the secretary's notes, are the official record of what transpired at the organization's meetings.

Minutes of a regular meeting are usually approved by general consent. However, a member may move that the minutes be approved as read. Minutes of a special meeting are read and approved at the next regular meeting. Minutes may be corrected whenever the error is noticed, even if it is months later. A member noticing the error can move to "amend something previously adopted." Only those who were present at a meeting can approve the minutes of that meeting.

Minutes for certain kinds of meetings may require special treatment. For example, the minutes of a convention usually are approved by the board or a special committee. Minutes of a board meeting may not be open for inspection by members unless the board grants permission; the board may instruct the secretary to give a summary of board actions at a regular meeting of the organization, however. The minutes of an executive session are read and acted upon only in the executive session. Finally, minutes generally are not kept in a small committee. The chair generally keeps complete notes of the proceedings, including options expressed, information gathered, and action taken.

There are a number of guidelines for most effectively keeping and presenting the minutes.

Format

The format of minutes varies with different organizations. However, minutes always are a brief summary of the proceedings of a meeting. They should be concise and sufficiently clear to be understood by a person not present at the meeting.

Minutes are evidence of what transpired at a meeting. After the reading and approval of the minutes, they become the official record of the transactions of the group. Therefore, the tone of the minutes should be impartial. Secretaries should be careful to avoid any personal comment. Members should be referred to by their titles, if any, or by their surnames.

Content

Minutes follow a regular order. The advantage to consistency is that members who are looking for information can find it easily.

The first paragraph of the minutes should specify the kind of meeting (regular, special, annual, adjourned); the name of the organization; the place, date, and hour; who was presiding and who was acting as secretary; attendance (by roll call, sign in, observation); and whether the minutes of the previous meeting were read and approved or mailed.

The body of the minutes should contain a separate paragraph for each subject. Some of the subjects in the body are

- Treasurer's report (read for information)

- Bills approved for payment

- Correspondence (read for information; if correspondence requires action, it should be read under new business)

- Condensed committee reports (entire reports may be attached)

It is often helpful to have a separate paragraph of the minutes for business transactions. Each paragraph should include the exact wording of the motion; the name of the person who made the motion; how the motion was acted upon or disposed of; and how the vote on the motion was taken. If a vote was counted, the minutes should include the number of votes for and against the motion.

Other items to be recorded in the minutes include:

- Names of persons appointed to committees
- All required notices
- Important announcements
- Names and subjects of speakers or participants at any program following the business
- Time of adjournment
- Secretary's signature

Common Mistakes in Preparing Minutes

There are a number of common errors that occur when secretaries are preparing the minutes of a meeting. One common error is the failure to show the complete wording of a motion. For example, poorly prepared minutes might read: "Mr. Johnson presented a resolution and moved its adoption. After amendment it was adopted as amended." A resolution is a substantive part of a motion. It should be recorded in the minutes as read by the member, and any amendments should be noted.

Another common mistake is the failure to show precise action taken on each motion made. The wording should clearly indicate how the motion was amended, if it was referred to a certain committee, or if it was postponed to the next meeting.

Still another common error is the failure to record important rulings. When a point of order is made, the chair makes a ruling that should be included in the minutes.

Another common mistake when preparing minutes is the failure to include complete, signed copies of all written reports presented at a meeting. Such items should be attached as numbered exhibits and legally made part of the minutes. References within the body of the minutes should state that such reports are attached.

Reading and Approval of Minutes

In organizations that hold weekly or monthly meetings, the minutes of the last meeting are the first item of business. Reading the minutes helps refresh the memories of those who were present and informs anyone who was absent.

The presiding officer calls upon the secretary to read the minutes. The secretary customarily rises to read them and remains standing while the president asks for corrections. If there are no corrections, the chair states that the minutes are approved as read. If there are corrections, the secretary makes the corrections in the margin.

Minutes are never rewritten after they have been read and corrected. If an error is pointed out and disputed, the secretary can refer to the notes or the presiding officer can take a vote to determine whether a mistake has been made. After the corrections have been completed, the president states that the minutes are approved as corrected. (A member also may move that the minutes be approved as corrected.) After approval, the secretary writes the word *approved* with the date, and signs or initials the minutes. The presiding officer may countersign.

In some organizations, the minutes are reproduced and sent to the members shortly after the meeting. This gives each member the information and the opportunity to correct any errors. If the minutes are mailed to the members, corrections can be made at the next meeting.

Dispensed Minutes

It may be necessary to dispense with the reading of the minutes. A motion can be made to dispense with the reading. This motion must be seconded. It is not debatable but can be amended. It requires a majority vote. If the presiding officer knows in advance that business must be attended to first, the presiding officer can say, "If there is no objection, the minutes will not be read at this time." He or she then waits and says, "Hearing no objection, the minutes will not be read." The reading of the minutes may be postponed to any later time during the meeting. If the minutes are not read at a given meeting, they must be read at the following meeting before the reading of the later minutes.

The reading of minutes should never be dispensed with unless a provision is made for correcting them.

Minute-Approving Committees

In order to save the time of reading lengthy minutes, a committee can be appointed or elected to approve the minutes. The committee has the responsibility for reading, correcting, and certifying the approval of the minutes. It is often a good idea to establish such a committee if the organization meets less than quarterly. Minutes should be approved by a committee when there is a different representation of delegates at the next meeting. A group of delegates cannot approve the minutes of a meeting they did not attend.

If the minutes will be approved by committee, committee members take their own notes at each meeting to serve as a check on the secretary's minutes. At the close of the meeting, the secretary sends a rough draft of the minutes to each committee member. The members check the minutes, make any necessary corrections, and sign and return them. The secretary makes the final draft of the minutes when all copies have been received. The secretary signs the minutes and adds "Approved by committee," listing the names of the committee members.

At the next meeting, the presiding officer states that the minutes have been approved by committee. However, a member can make a motion to have the minutes read.

Chapter 4

The Members

A member of an organization has associational rights. These rights differ in each organization according to how they are provided for in the bylaws of the organization. To assert rights, a member must choose the proper time and follow the proper procedure.

Unless otherwise stated in the bylaws, members usually are responsible for the approval of matters pertaining to the policies, program, budget, and election of the officers and directors.

Since all members are seldom present at every meeting, it is necessary to allow a certain proportion of the membership to transact the business of the organization. This proportion of the membership is called the *quorum*. A quorum is the minimum number of voting members who must be present at a meeting in order for business to be legally transacted. A quorum always refers to the number present and not to the number actually voting. The number which constitutes a quorum should be provided for in the bylaws.

Duties of the Members

Members of any organization have special duties. Specific duties are spelled out by the organization's bylaws. However, some general duties are required of members of any body.

The first general duty of any member is to be familiar with the rules and customs of the organization. Members should keep the goals of the organization in mind. They should always follow the organization's guidelines for achieving those goals. If there are goals or guidelines that seem counterproductive, an informed member will know the organization's policies for making constructive changes.

Any time the organization convenes, members are responsible for keeping meetings running smoothly. Members always should pay close attention to speakers and to the business at hand. Remarks should be confined to the question before the assembly. Members should address all remarks to and through the presiding officer —not to other members.

A fundamental understanding of parliamentary procedure is very helpful to all members of an organization. Parliamentary procedure not only governs the mechanics of a meeting, it also ensures that members' rights are upheld. Every member should know the basic steps in presenting a motion. Every member also should know some of the most helpful motions—such as those that allow a member to ask a question.

Members also have a general duty to abstain from making remarks outside a meeting that might in any way interfere with the work being done by an officer or committee. Basically, members should make sure that their actions and remarks further the objectives of the organization.

Rights of the Members

Parliamentary law is built on rights: rights of the majority, rights of the minority, rights of individuals, and rights of absentees. Every member is responsible for seeing that these rights are respected.

When a person joins an organization, she or he acquires certain rights that are spelled out in the bylaws. There are also some fundamental rights.

Members have the right to receive notice of when meetings will be held and to attend those meetings. They also have the right to expect that meetings will begin on time and be properly conducted.

At any meeting, members have the right to explain or discuss motions that they present. Similarly, they have the right to discuss motions presented by others. Members have the right to speak without interruption, subject to the rules applicable to all members of the organization. They also have the right to request additional information from the presiding officer or to ask for an explanation of any pending question that is not understood.

Parliamentary procedure allows for some special cases in discussion. For example, if a motion contains two or more distinct propositions, each of which is capable of standing alone, members can ask to have the question divided. If the presiding officer has made a ruling that at least two members disagree with, the members have the right to appeal the ruling of the chair. The members also have the right to raise a point of order when the presiding officer does not notice a mistake or omission.

Generally, all members have the right to nominate and to be nominated for office. They also have the right to vote or to abstain from voting—although members who do not vote have the effect of silently voting with the prevailing side. Members should vote for themselves when they are candidates for office. They also have the right to serve on committees.

Some other rights of members include:

- The right to resign if all obligations to the organization have been fulfilled

- The right to have a hearing before expulsion or other penalty

- The right to inspect official records of the organization in the presence of an officer

- The right to insist on enforcement of the rules of the organization

Regulations

In any meeting, with the rights of membership come certain procedural responsibilities.

A member can be ruled *out of order* for the following reasons:

1. Addressing another member instead of the chair in a debate.

2. Using the names of members in debate.

3. Failing to confine remarks to the merits of the pending question.

4. Persisting in speaking on irrelevant matters.

5. Making a motion and then speaking against it.

6. Speaking without first having risen, addressed the chair, and obtained the floor.

7. Speaking longer than permitted by the rules of the body.

8. Stating in debate that another's statement is false. (It is acceptable to say that another is mistaken.)

9. Disturbing the assembly, such as by whispering or walking across the room.

Parliamentary Pointers for the Members

A member who is better informed will participate more confidently in debate and will be better respected by other members. A few pointers will help any member feel and sound in command of parliamentary procedure.

Parliamentary Phrases

How something is phrased often separates the savvy member from the one who is uncertain about parliamentary procedure.

When addressing the chair, any of the following are acceptable:

- Madam President—Mr. President

- Mr. Chair—Madam Chair

- Madam Moderator—Mr. Moderator

The correct way to begin a motion is with the words "I move that"—not "I motion that" or "I make a motion to." Motions always should be stated in the affirmative. It often is possible to express a negative idea in affirmative words. For example, "I move that we do not solicit funds for the convention" uses negative wording and is objectionable. The motion could be phrased, "I move that the funds for the convention be unsolicited."

The correct phrasing for a number of helpful parliamentary procedures is listed in Table 3.1.

Table 3.1

Parliamentary Phrases for the Members

Motions

- I move to amend the motion by . . . .
- I speak in favor of the motion . . . .
- I speak in opposition to the motion . . . .
- I object to the consideration of the motion (*or* resolution).
- I move to suspend the rules to take up . . . .

Voting

- Is there a quorum present?
- Division. *or* I call for a counted vote.

Debate

- I rise to a point of information.
- I rise to a parliamentary inquiry.
- I rise to a point of order.
- I appeal from the decision of the chair.
- Madam (*or* Mr.) President, will the member yield for a question?

Who May Speak

The first person who rises and asks for recognition when no member has the floor is entitled to be recognized. When two or more members rise to claim the floor, the member who rose and addressed the chair first is entitled to be recognized. When several members seek recognition at the same time, three basic rules help decide which member should be recognized.

First, preference is given to the proposer of a motion or to the committee chair who has presented a report. The person who made the motion is allowed to speak first to the motion. The person who made the report should be allowed to speak first to the committee's recommendations.

Second, a member who has not spoken has prior claim over one who has already discussed the question. This insures that as many views as possible are aired during every debate.

Third, debate should alternate between proponents and opponents of a motion. The chair may inquire which position a member will present.

In some cases, members may wish to interrupt speakers. Parliamentary procedure includes several motions that enable a member to interrupt debate. Such motions include:

- Point of order

- Question of privilege

- Point of no quorum

- Call for the orders of the day

- Appeal from the decision of the chair

- Parliamentary inquiry

- Question of information

- Give notice of information

- Objection to the consideration of a question
- Motion to divide a motion

Although this discussion has addressed when a member may speak, parliamentary procedure also addresses members who do not speak. Members who remain silent when presumably aware that they have been named to a duty are regarded as accepting that duty. They thereby place themselves under the same obligations as if they had accepted verbally.

Change of Vote

Members are permitted to change their votes. Change of vote is acceptable when the vote is taken by show of hands, voice, roll call, or standing. With a written ballot, change of vote is not possible, since there is no way to show how the member voted the first time.

To change a vote, a member might say the following: "I ask permission to change my vote from *Aye* to *No*." If no one objects when asked by the presiding officer, permission is granted. If someone objects—simply by calling out "Objection"—the member may move that he or she be permitted to change the vote. The motion must be seconded, and a majority vote is required to approve the change.

Members may change their votes only between the time they vote and the time the chair announces the result. When the chair says "The motion is carried" or "The motion is defeated," members lose the chance to change their votes without the permission of the assembly.

Chapter 5

Motions

Business is transacted in a meeting by way of motions. A member makes a proposal that is accepted or rejected. The members of the assembly may wish to defer consideration of the subject, or they may be willing to accept it with certain modifications.

Kinds of Motions

There are two kinds of motions: *main* and *secondary*. The main motion is the proposal or proposition. If the main motion is accepted, it commits the assembly to take action. The main motion has implications beyond the present meeting.

Motions are classified in the following ways:

I. Main Motions
   A. Original
   B. Specific Main Motions

II. Secondary Motions
   A. Subsidiary
   B. Privileged
   C. Incidental

The main motion brings business before the assembly. A secondary motion is a procedural motion that is made and considered while the main motion is on the floor. When a secondary motion is made, it becomes the immediately pending question, while the main motion remains pending. Certain secondary motions take priority over others. It is possible to have more than one secondary motion pending at the same time that the main motion is pending.

Main Motions

A main motion is a proposal that brings business before the assembly. The proposal is a member's request that something be done or that a statement express the sense, opinion, or wish of the assembly. As a general rule, a main motion is stated in the affirmative. It should be clear, definite, and brief. A long or complicated motion should be submitted in writing.

Parliamentary procedure governs how a motion should be presented and when it is in order. A main motion requires recognition by the chair, requires a second, is debatable, and is amendable. A main motion is not in order when another member has the floor. It yields to any subsidiary, privileged, or applicable incidental motion.

A main motion usually requires a majority vote. Exceptions to this rule include when the bylaws of the organization require a greater vote, when adoption would suspend a rule of order or a parliamentary right, or when adoption would rescind or amend something previously adopted. A main motion may be reconsidered by the assembly.

All subsidiary and privileged motions can be made while the main motion is pending. Other applicable incidental motions can be made, for example, division of the question, to consider seriatim (consider the proposition paragraph by paragraph), to withdraw, and to object to the consideration of an original main motion.

Specific main motions are motions that are incidental to or relate to the business of the assembly or to its past or future action. They usually are made orally. Some examples of specific main motions include:

- To ratify emergency action taken at a meeting when no quorum was present

- To rescind an action or rule already adopted

- To adopt a recommendation that an officer or committee has been directed to make

- To take a motion laid on the table from the table

- To amend something previously adopted

A member may object to the consideration of an original main motion, but it is not in order to object to the consideration of an incidental main motion.

Resolutions

A *resolution* is a formally written main motion. It may be a formal statement of the opinions of the assembly.

The difference between a standard main motion and a resolution is that a main motion is proposed by the words "I move that . . . ." A resolution is proposed by the words "I move the adoption of the following resolution,

Resolved, That . . . ." A resolution presented by a committee or board does not require a second, but all other rules pertaining to a main motion apply.

A resolution may have a *preamble*. A preamble consists of one or more clauses, each beginning with the word *Whereas*. The preamble is a brief statement giving the background or reasons for the motion. It presents arguments for the resolution's adoption. The preamble should contain only clauses that contain little-known information or items of unusual importance, without which the resolution is likely to be misunderstood.

The correct format for a resolution is illustrated below. In the preamble, the word *Whereas* introduces each item. It is followed by a comma. The next word begins with a capital letter, and the phrase ends with a semicolon followed by the word *and*. The last *Whereas* closes with a semicolon followed by the words *therefore be it* or simply *be it*. The beginning resolving clause begins a new line.

Whereas, A . . . ; and
Whereas, The . . .; therefore be it
Resolved, That [stating action to be taken]; and
Resolved, That [stating further action to be taken].

Each resolving clause in a resolution is voted on separately, as each is a primary motion. Each clause may be debated, amended, referred, postponed, or laid on the table. After the resolving clauses have been voted upon, the preamble is then put to a vote. Depending on the disposition of the resolving clauses, the preamble may be amended.

Courtesy Resolution

A committee is often charged with the duty of drafting and presenting to the assembly a *courtesy resolution*. Ordinarily, courtesy resolutions express the appreciation of an assembly or convention to those who arranged accommodations or rendered service. No opposing vote is taken on a courtesy resolution.

Subsidiary Motions

Subsidiary motions assist in treating or disposing of the main motion or other motions. They are used to modify, delay action on, or dispose of the pending motion. When a subsidiary motion is stated by the chair, it supersedes a pending motion of lower rank and becomes the immediately pending question.

Certain subsidiary motions may be applied to others. For example, a motion to amend may be amended, referred to a committee, or postponed. Debate on an amendment may be limited or extended by subsidiary motion.

Subsidiary motions, their purpose, and their application are discussed in depth in the Appendix "Handbook of Useful Motions," beginning on page 73.

Precedence of Motions

Before a subject can be considered, it must be brought before the assembly in the form of a motion or proposition. Only one main motion can be considered at a time. After the main motion has been stated by the chair, it must be adopted or rejected by the assembly, or the assembly must take some other action to dispose of it before any other subject can be brought up.

The consideration of a main motion may involve a number of secondary motions. Secondary motions enable an assembly to arrive at the general will of the members on a number of questions. The presiding officer is responsible for recognizing a secondary motion, its purpose, and its rank. The presiding officer should ensure that motions are handled in their proper order of precedence. Table 5.1 lists the various kinds of motions and shows their precedence.

Table 5.1
Table of Motions

	Can Interrupt Speaker	Requires Second	Debatable	Amendable	Vote Required	Can Be Reconsidered
Privileged Motions						
Fix the time to which to adjourn	no	yes	no	yes	majority	yes
Adjourn (unqualified)	no	yes	no	no	majority	no
Take a recess	no	yes	no	yes	majority	no
Question of privilege	yes	no	no	no	•	no
Orders of the day	yes	no	no	no	•	no
Subsidiary Motions						
Lay on the table (temporarily)	no	yes	no	no	majority	no
Previous question (stop debate)	no	yes	no	no	2/3	yes
Limit or extend debate	no	yes	no	yes	2/3	yes
Postpone to certain time	no	yes	yes	yes	majority	yes

* Except when the motion to be reconsidered is debatable.
• Chair usually decides. Majority if put to vote.
(1) Requires a two-thirds vote when applied to constitution, bylaws, or special rules. Requires a majority vote when notice is given at a previous meeting, or a majority vote of the entire membership without notice.
(2) If not granted by general consent, can be moved by person requesting permission.
(3) Yes, if motion made by person requesting permission.

	Can Interrupt Speaker	Requires Second	Debatable	Amendable	Vote Required	Can Be Reconsidered
Refer to committee	no	yes	yes	yes	majority	yes
Amend	no	yes	yes	yes	majority	yes
Postpone indefinitely	no	yes	yes	no	majority	aff. vote only
Main Motion	no	yes	yes	yes	majority	yes
Specific Main Motions						
Reconsider	no	yes	yes*	no	majority	no
Ratify	no	yes	yes	yes	majority	yes
Rescind	no	yes	yes	yes	(1)	neg. vote only
Take from the table	no	yes	no	no	majority	no
Discharge committee	no	yes	yes	yes	2/3	neg. vote only
Amend something previously adopted	no	yes	yes	yes	(1)	neg. vote only

	Can Interrupt Speaker	Requires Second	Debatable	Amendable	Vote Required	Can Be Reconsidered
Incidental Motions (no rank)						
Point of order	yes	no	no	no	●	no
Appeal from the decision of chair	yes	yes	limited	no	majority	yes
Suspend the rules of order	no	yes	no	no	2/3	no
Suspend standing rules	no	yes	no	no	majority	no
Object to consideration	yes	no	no	no	2/3	neg. vote only
Division of a question (motion)	no	yes	no	yes	majority	no
Consider by paragraph (section)	no	yes	no	yes	majority	no
Division of assembly (vote)	yes	no	no	no	none	no
Close polls	no	yes	no	yes	2/3	no

* Except when the motion to be reconsidered is debatable.
● Chair usually decides. Majority if put to vote.
(1) Requires a two-thirds vote when applied to constitution, bylaws, or special rules. Requires a majority vote when notice is given at a previous meeting, or a majority vote of the entire membership without notice.
(2) If not granted by general consent, can be moved by person requesting permission.
(3) Yes, if motion made by person requesting permission.

	Can Interrupt Speaker	Requires Second	Debatable	Amendable	Vote Required	Can Be Reconsidered
Reopen polls	no	yes	no	yes	majority	neg. vote only
Close nominations	no	yes	no	yes	2/3	no
Reopen nominations	no	yes	no	yes	majority	neg. vote only
Parliamentary inquiry	yes	no	no	no	none	no
Request for information	yes	no	no	no	none	no
Excused for duty	no	yes	yes	yes	majority	neg. vote only
Withdraw a motion	(1)	(2)	no	no	majority	neg. vote only
Create a blank	no	yes	no	no	majority	no
Fill a blank	no	no	yes	no	majority	yes
Request to read a paper	(1)	(2)	no	no	majority	yes
Motions relating to voting	no	yes	no	yes	majority	no

* Except when the motion to be reconsidered is debatable.

• Chair usually decides. Majority if put to vote.

(1) Requires a two-thirds vote when applied to constitution, bylaws, or special rules. Requires a majority vote when notice is given at a previous meeting, or a majority vote of the entire membership without notice.

(2) If not granted by general consent, can be moved by person requesting permission.

(3) Yes, if motion made by person requesting permission.

Chapter 6

Nominations and Elections

The method of nominating and electing officers should be specified in the bylaws of the organization. If no method is prescribed in the bylaws, a member may move that nominations be made by the chair, by a committee, by ballot, or that they be taken from the floor.

A *nomination* is a proposal that a certain position be filled. It is an assurance that the nominee will serve in the specified office if elected. One who seeks an office is a *candidate*. When the candidate's name is put up for nomination, he or she is then a *nominee*.

Nominations

A member cannot nominate more than one person for an office until all members have had an opportunity to nominate someone. A nomination does not require a second.

Nominations cannot be amended; however, a nominating speech may be given.

No motion is necessary to close nominations. The chair simply declares that nominations are closed. However, if a motion is made to close nominations, the motion requires a two-thirds vote. Nominations may be reopened by a majority vote.

If a person is nominated and unable or unwilling to serve, he or she should decline immediately. The same person can be nominated for more than one office. However, if elected to more than one office, the person must decide in which office she or he will serve. If the person is absent from the actual election, the assembly must decide which office that person will fill.

Nominations by the Chair

The chair may nominate committee members. A member can move to amend by striking out certain names. The chair then nominates another to take the place of the one stricken out. A majority vote is taken on all the nominees.

Nominations by Committee

In an election of officers, nominations usually are made by a *nominating committee*. Usually the bylaws of the organization specify if the committee is elected or appointed. The committee may be a standing committee, or it may be a special committee elected in advance of the officer election.

Members on the nominating committee should represent the various interest groups in the organization. The president should have no part in the selection of the committee, nor be an ex-officio member of it.

The nominating committee members should be familiar with the membership and the organization bylaws that describe the nominating procedures. By studying the needs of the organization, the committee can prepare a list of potential officers who can work together well and represent different groups within the organization. Several questions should be considered in the committee meeting:

1. Does the person being considered believe in the objectives of the organization?

2. Does the person have the time to devote to the duties of the office?

3. Does the person have a good relationship with others in the organization?

4. What has been the past performance of the person?

When preparing to select nominees, the nominating committee should request a current membership list and an attendance record from the secretary of the organization. Members of the organization may suggest names of prospective nominees for the committee's review. A member of the nominating committee may be considered as a candidate. It is not necessary for the member to resign from the committee.

When the committee agrees on a prospective candidate, the candidate should be contacted while the committee is still in session to make sure she or he will serve if nominated and elected. No prospective candidate should be contacted by an individual committee member prior to the committee meeting. Once selected and contacted, the committee must have the candidate's agreement to serve before that person's name is included in the committee report. Some organizations require that such an agreement be signed before an individual is included as a candidate.

The number of nominees for each office depends on the bylaws of the organization. Unless the bylaws state otherwise, the committee is only required to submit one candidate for each office to be filled. Selection of a candidate should be by majority vote.

The information discussed in committee is confidential. The nominating committee should make every effort to weigh the qualifications and responsibilities of each person and of the office. The committee's candidate should be the individual best suited to the position.

Committee Report

After a majority of the committee has agreed on the nominees, a report is made and signed by all members who agree on it. The report is read to the assembly by the committee chair at the request of the presiding officer. It is then given to the presiding officer or the secretary. The report is not accepted or adopted by the members.

After the report has been read, the committee is automatically discharged. It can be recalled if a nominee withdraws (or declines) before the election. If the committee's nominee is elected and then resigns, the vacancy is filled by the prescribed method in the bylaws.

Voting by Ballot

The nominating ballot is usually prepared by the nominating committee. The nominating committee prepares a ballot containing the names of the nominees and space for nominations from the floor or write-in candidates. The ballot is given to each voting member. The chair then instructs the members how to mark and fold the ballot.

When the balloting is completed, the chair directs the *tellers* to collect the ballots. Tellers are responsible for ensuring that the balloting proceeds smoothly and that no member votes more than once. Because of this, ballots should not simply be passed to the center isle. When only voters are present, members can remain in their seats and drop their ballots into a receptacle passed by one teller and checked by another teller. An alternative method is to have members go to a central ballot box and deposit their ballots. Ballots also can be handed to a teller, who then deposits them in a central box.

Nominations from the Floor

The procedure for taking nominations from the floor is fairly simple. The presiding officer states that nominations are in order for a particular office. It is then in order for any member to make a nomination for the office. Generally, when the chair calls for nominations from the floor, a member need not rise and be recognized by the chair. However, in a large meeting or a convention, members should rise.

When making a nomination, the member should state, "I nominate Member Alvarez." The chair then repeats the nomination ("Member Alvarez has been nominated") and asks for further nominations. When all nominations have been made, the chair closes the nominations. A motion is not necessary; however, if a member does move to close nominations, the motion must be seconded and requires a two-thirds vote.

It is possible to reopen nominations after they have been closed. The member should rise, wait for recognition by the chair, and then state, "I move that nominations be reopened for the office of . . . ." The motion must be seconded. It is not debatable, but it may be amended. The chair then calls for a voice vote to reopen the nominations. If the vote is in the affirmative, the chair calls for further nominations.

After nominations have been closed, voting for that office takes place, or nominations for the next office can be called for by the chair.

Elections

Each organization should adopt the method of electing officers best suited to the organization. This method should be spelled out in the bylaws, and all required formalities should be observed. For example, if the bylaws require an election to be by ballot, a motion to dispense with the ballot is illegal. Similarly, the secretary may be instructed to cast the elective ballot only if provided for in the bylaws.

When only one candidate is nominated for an office, provision should be included for a simple method of election. Generally, if a candidate is unopposed and the bylaws do not require election to be by ballot, the chair may call for a voice vote.

When it appears that everyone has voted, the chair closes the polls. A majority vote is required to elect a nominee to office. A single vote may be considered a majority vote if it is the only vote cast. A *plurality vote* (largest number of votes cast) does not elect, unless provided for in the bylaws or by a specially adopted rule.

An election becomes final immediately if the candidate is present and did not decline the nomination. If the candidate is absent and has not consented to the nomination, the election becomes final when she or he is notified of the election and does not decline.

Tellers

In addition to distributing, collecting, and counting ballots, tellers are appointed by the chair to report the vote. It is the tellers' responsibility to see that no member votes more than once. The number of tellers varies with the number of voters. (A minimum of two or three is advised.) Tellers are chosen for accuracy and dependability. They should not be personally involved in the election.

Tellers' Procedure

Tellers distribute ballots to those entitled to vote in the election. After the presiding officer declares the voting closed, the ballots are collected and then counted. The counting preferably takes place in another room. When counting the ballots, tellers should make certain that the number of ballots is equal to or less than the number of eligible voters.

Tally sheets should be used to count the votes. They should be prepared by the tellers when nominations are complete. A minimum of four tellers is advisable, so that one teller can serve as a check on the other. If there are four tellers, the first teller opens the ballot, the second teller reads the ballot aloud, and the third and fourth tellers mark their tally sheets.

Tally sheets are marked with vertical lines in groups of four, with a fifth mark going diagonally across the four vertical lines. When a teller makes the fifth mark, he or she calls out "Tally." The other tellers should be in agreement. If they do not agree, they should recheck the last five ballots.

When tallying votes, blank ballots are not counted. Misspelled words or names are counted if the meaning is clear. Illegal votes are recorded separately. When all votes have been tallied, the tellers' report is compiled in duplicate (see Figure 6.1 for sample tellers' report). The tally sheets are sealed in an envelope. Tally sheets should be retained until there is no possibility of them being required again; they should then be destroyed.

The tellers return to the assembly and present their report when called upon. The chair of the tellers reads the report and then presents it to the president, who announces the results. Because votes are confidential, tellers may not divulge the vote of anyone whose ballot they recognized.

Figure 6.1

Sample Tellers' Report

1. The number eligible to vote _____

2. The number of votes cast _____

3. The number of votes necessary to elect _____

4. The number of votes received by each candidate

Candidate	Number of Votes
_____	_____
_____	_____
_____	_____
_____	_____

5. Illegal votes _____

Chapter 7

Bylaws and Standing Rules

The *bylaws* of an organization are the rules adopted by the members to regulate and manage the organization's business and to set forth the rights and duties of its members. They also define the specific duties and responsibilities of directors and elected officers. The bylaws of membership organizations vary, depending on the objectives of the organization.

Bylaws have a direct bearing on the rights of members within an organization. Every member should be given a copy of the bylaws to study. When a member joins an organization, that member agrees to abide by its bylaws.

Content of Bylaws

Everything relating to a subject should be placed in the same or adjacent article of the bylaws. Each article may have several subdivisions. Nothing in the bylaws should conflict with other articles.

Expressions used in bylaws should be clear. For example, under an article on officers, if the term of office is stated as "one year," at the end of one year the term expires, whether or not a successor has been elected. However, by using the expression "one year and/or until the successor is elected," the officer holds over until the successor is elected. If *or* is used, the organization has a right to declare an office vacant by the same vote required to rescind any action taken. If *and* is used, the organization cannot vacate an office.

Bylaws are prepared by a committee. It is the committee's function to make certain that the bylaw provisions do not conflict with the actual operating procedures and objectives of the organization. A bylaws committee should include the persons interested, as well as those who are likely to spend much time in discussing the bylaws. After the large committee has had one or two meetings on the subject and has come to an agreement, it should appoint a subcommittee of two or three persons to actually write the bylaws.

Structure of Bylaws

Bylaws provide the legal framework within which the organization functions. Bylaws are divided into *articles* assigned with Roman numerals. Each article is subdivided into *sections*, or paragraphs, in which Arabic numerals are assigned. By convention, the word *article* should be placed in the center of the page and the word *section* to the left of the page.

The standard pattern for bylaws is illustrated in Figure 7.1. Usually the name of the organization is the first article, the object or purpose of the organization is the second article, and subsequent articles have to do with membership, finances, officers, meetings, and such. It is helpful to have an article that deals with the bylaws themselves, so that members know the proper procedure for amendments.

Presenting the Bylaws

After the proposed bylaws have been examined by the bylaws committee, and no inconsistencies or ambiguities exist, they should be typed and circulated to the membership well in advance of the meeting at which they are to be voted on. Copies should be shown ahead of time to the parliamentarian and other legal advisors so that any legal or technical questions can be resolved.

At the voting meeting, the presiding officer calls on the bylaws committee to report. The committee chair says, "By direction of the committee, I move the adoption of the proposed bylaws." No second is necessary.

The bylaws then are read, one article or section at a time. Each article or section is then open to debate and amendment. When amendment of one section is complete, the next is considered.

After the last article has been completed, the chair asks for any further amendments. If there are any, they are considered. When all the amendments are complete, the chair asks for a vote on the adoption of the bylaws as amended. Normally, bylaws are adopted by a two-thirds vote. If bylaws are being adopted for the first time, only a majority vote is necessary. The vote may be taken by voice.

Amendments to Bylaws

After a period of time it may be necessary to amend portions of the bylaws. The motion to amend the bylaws is an incidental main motion. It is subject to the same rules as a main motion, except that the vote required for its adoption is specified in the bylaws. A proposed amendment may be amended by a majority vote.

A proposed amendment to the bylaws should be stated in language that, if adopted, may be incorporated directly into the bylaws. Some organizations provide that the proposed amendment be given to the bylaws committee for study. The committee then reports its recommendations to the voting members. When reporting, the committee should fully explain every section, and explain the changes that will result from the proposed change.

Amendment Procedures

Parliamentary procedure governs certain elements of amending bylaws. First, no amendment is in order that increases the modification of the article or rule to be amended. Second, in an amendment to strike out a sentence, paragraph, or section, the existing bylaw itself is not open to consideration, only the amendment to the bylaw.

Next, an amendment to the bylaws goes into effect immediately with the announcement of the vote adopting it, unless the motion to adopt provides that it become effective at a later time.

Fourth, to change the quorum provision in the bylaws, the proper procedure is to strike out and insert the new provision in one sentence and to vote on it as one question.

Finally, an amendment or motion to change the number of sections or paragraphs is not necessary. The secretary makes such corrections as they become necessary.

The procedure for amending the bylaws should be set forth in the bylaws. The power to amend the bylaws lies primarily with the membership as a whole. However, this power may be delegated to the board of directors, unless prohibited by the bylaws or articles of incorporation.

Revising Bylaws

When changes in the bylaws are extensive and scattered throughout, a substitution should be made with an entirely new set of bylaws. Amending bylaws by substitution is called a *revision*. The best method is to select a special committee for this purpose, or the bylaws committee may submit a revision.

A copy of the proposed revision with the date it will be considered and voted upon should be sent to each member in advance of the meeting. It is considered and voted upon under the same procedure that is followed for adopting the original bylaws. Each article is discussed and any amendments are acted upon at that time. Each amendment requires a majority vote. When there are no further amendments nor any further discussion, a counted standing vote is taken.

A revised set of bylaws becomes effective immediately after the vote adopting the new revision. However, it is possible to adopt a motion to provide that certain portions of the revised bylaws should not become effective until a specified time.

Standing Rules

An organization's *standing rules* usually relate to administrative details. Any adopted main motion which has continuing effects is a standing rule. It continues in force until it is rescinded. Examples of standing rules include: time for the meeting to begin; location of the meeting; policy concerning guests; and responsibilities for refreshments. Standing rules are adopted as the need arises at any business meeting. No previous notice is necessary.

Standing rules for a convention are not the same as the standing rules for the organization. A committee generally prepares the proposed rules that cover such subjects as seating of delegates and alternates, length of speeches, and privileges of nonvoting members. While these rules apply only to a particular convention, they may be held over to another convention with only slight changes.

After the convention rules committee reports, the rules may be debated or amended. A single member may ask for a separate vote on any individual rule. The rules usually are adopted as a whole by a two-thirds vote. During the convention, any standing rule can be suspended by a majority vote.

Figure 7.1

Basic Pattern for Bylaws

ARTICLE I

NAME

1. Give full, exact name, properly punctuated

2. Name should have some relationship to the purpose and function of the organization

3. Name should be clearly understood

ARTICLE II

OBJECT *or* PURPOSE

1. May be expressed in a single sentence

2. May be specified in a series of descriptive phrases set off by semicolons

3. Each statement should be clearly worked out so that it cannot be misinterpreted

4. Serves as the basic authority for future actions of the organization

ARTICLE III

MEMBERS

1. Classes of membership (active, associate, sustaining, firm, life, inactive, honorary, emeritus, family)

   a. Rights of each class (distinction between classes; limitations on number; family membership—can husband and wife have joint membership; age limit for children voting)

---

2. Qualifications for membership

   a. Limited to those in a certain geographical area?

   b. How are members admitted? (invitation, sponsor, credit rating, ethnic background, age, other)

3. Procedure for applying for membership

   a. Approved application? (what questions are included)

   b. Time schedule for handling applications (including time limitations for reaching a decision about applications)

4. Termination of membership

5. Rights of members (to hold office, participate in functions and activities)

6. Resignation of membership

7. Transfer of membership

8. Honorary members and officers

ARTICLE IV

FINANCES

1. Required dues and fees

2. Date payable (annually, quarterly)

3. Do fees and dues vary for different classes of membership?

4. Time and procedure for notifying members if they become delinquent in payment

5. Penalties for nonpayment

6. Date when member will be dropped for nonpayment

7. Does a delinquent member maintain voting rights?

8. Does the organization have the right and power to assess members additional sums on top of dues?

9. Fiscal year and membership year

10. Conference or convention expenses for officers

11. Bond for treasurer

12. Check authorization and endorsement (how many officers, which ones)

13. Audit

14. Budget (when presented)

ARTICLE V

OFFICERS

1. Title and number of officers

2. Qualifications

3. Term of office and powers of each officer

4. Duties of each officer (which duties will be handled by officers and which duties by committees)

5. Vacancies (how filled)

6. Appointed officers

7. Directors

   a. Term of office

   b. How elected

   c. How many

ARTICLE VI

NOMINATIONS and ELECTIONS

1. Nominating committee

   a. When appointed or elected?

   b. Number of terms a member may serve

c. Eligibility of members (from different regions?)

d. Duties

e. Required number of nominees for each office

f. Nominations from floor

g. When to report

h. Rules governing nominees

2. Elections

   a. When? (first order of business?)

   b. By ballot (procedure to follow if candidate does not receive a majority vote)

   c. By mail (describe procedure)

   d. By proxy (describe procedure)

   e. By voice if only one candidate, or chair declare the candidate elected

ARTICLE VII

MEETINGS

1. Kinds of meetings

   a. Regular (day on which meeting is held; the hour should be in the standing rules)

   b. Special (who may call a special meeting; how far in advance notice must be given; how members are notified)

   c. Annual (for the purpose of hearing annual reports, conducting elections; time, place, notice of meeting)

2. Quorum

ARTICLE VIII

(The title of this article may vary. Options include: Executive Committee; Board of Directors; Councils; Board of Governors; Board of Managers; Board of Trustees)

1. Composition (qualifications, term of office)

2. Powers

   a. Full power and authority over affairs of the organization (with certain exceptions)

   b. Does the board control the whole organization?

   c. Does the board have limited power to act for the organization between meetings?

   d. Specific powers (to elect their own officers, fill vacancies, discharge employees of the organization)

   e. Review and termination of memberships for cause

   f. Purchasing power, selling or lease of property

3. Meetings of the board

   a. How often? (notice to be given)

   b. Right of an ordinary member to be informed of board activities

   c. Report to the membership

   d. How special meetings are called

   e. Do repeated absences constitute an automatic resignation?

   f. How are vacancies filled?

4. Quorum

ARTICLE IX

COMMITTEES

1. Standing committees listed by name (no other committees can be added without amending the bylaws; list all essential committees)

   a. Composition of the committee

   b. Vacancies, quorum

   c. Manner of selecting members for the committee

   d. Shall the president be an ex-officio member?

2. Special committees (ad hoc)

   a. How elected or appointed

   b. Duties and powers

ARTICLE X

(At this place other articles may be added. Suggested articles include: Conventions; Regions; Councils; Discipline; Seal or Emblem; Indemnification; Publications; Headquarters. Each should be in a separate article. There should be a separate article on Dissolution to meet the requirements of the IRS.)

(Next to the last ARTICLE)

PARLIAMENTARY AUTHORITY

(State the parliamentary authority that is to be the guide on all matters not covered by the organization's charter, bylaws, or standing rules.)

(Always the last ARTICLE)

AMENDMENTS TO BYLAWS

1. How changes are to be made (by committee, by individual member of the organization)

2. Notice of the amendment

   a. In writing (form in which proposed amendments are to be stated)

   b. How far in advance (required notice to all members; notice given at *a* previous meeting is not the same as *the* previous meeting)

3. Procedure for approving an amendment

4. Vote required (voice, ballot, mail)

5. Emergency procedures (disaster preventing the holding of a convention or national catastrophe)

Appendix

Handbook of Useful Motions

This appendix covers the most commonly used motions, their purpose, and their application. The appendix is arranged in alphabetical order for easy reference.

There are two kinds of motions, *main* and *secondary*. Main motions are the motions that bring business before the meeting. Secondary motions are procedural and can be considered while a main motion is on the floor. Secondary motions are identified as subsidiary, privileged, and incidental.

Subsidiary motions are always applied to another motion while it is pending and, if adopted, always do something to this other motion. Subsidiary motions have rank. When a motion is before the meeting, any motion is in order if it has a higher precedence or rank than the immediately pending motion; no motion having a lower precedence is in order.

Privileged motions deal with special matters of immediate importance which, without debate, are allowed to interrupt the consideration of anything else. They have no bearing on the subject before the meeting.

Incidental motions apply to the method of transacting business, rather than to the business itself. They relate in different ways to the pending business and deal with questions of procedure arising out of another pending motion. Incidental motions have no rank among themselves. With few exceptions, they are related to the main question in such a way that they must be decided upon immediately, before any business can proceed.

There can be only one main motion on the floor at a time, but it is possible to have several secondary motions on the floor at the same time, provided they are made according to their rank.

Table A.1 lists the order of precedence of motions.

Table A.1

Order of Precedence of Motions—Highest to Lowest

I.   Privileged Motions

    1. Fix the Time to Which to Adjourn

    2. Adjourn

    3. Recess

    4. Question of Privilege

    5. Call for the Orders of the Day

II.   Subsidiary Motions

    6. Lay on the Table

    7. Previous Question

    8. Limit or Extend Debate

    9. Postpone Definitely

   10. Commit or Refer

   11. Amend

   12. Postpone Indefinitely

III.   The Main Motion

IV.   Specific Main Motions (no order of precedence)

    Discharge a Committee

    Ratify

    Reconsider

    Rescind

    Take from the Table

V.   Incidental Motions (no order of procedence)

Appeal

Consider by Paragraph or Seriatim

Division of a Question

Division of the Assembly

Motions Relating to Nominations

Motions Relating to the Polls and Methods of
Voting

Motions That Are Requests

Object to the Consideration of a Question

Point of Order

Suspend the Rules

Withdraw

Adjourn

A privileged motion. This motion is made to terminate a
meeting.

Forms of the Motion

"I move that we adjourn."

"I move to adjourn."

"I move that we adjourn at 8 o'clock."

"I move that when we adjourn, we adjourn to meet at
the same time tomorrow evening."

Rules Governing the Motion

1. Cannot interrupt a speaker
2. Requires recognition
3. Is not debatable
4. Is not amendable
5. Requires a majority vote
6. May not be reconsidered

After the motion to adjourn has been moved, the following parliamentary steps are in order while the motion to adjourn is pending, or after the meeting has voted to adjourn:

1. Inform the members of business requiring attention before adjournment
2. Make important announcements
3. Make (but not take up) a motion to reconsider a previous vote
4. Give notice of a motion to be made at the next meeting (or on the next day of a convention) where the motion requires previous notice
5. Move to set the time for an adjourned meeting if the time for the next meeting is not already settled

The meeting is not closed until the chair has declared that the meeting is adjourned. Members should not leave their seats until the chair says, "The meeting is adjourned."

A meeting can be adjourned without a motion if the time for adjournment has arrived. The chair simply announces that the meeting is adjourned. When it appears that there is no further business, the chair may say, "There being no further business, the meeting is adjourned."

Adopt

An incidental motion. The expressions *adopt, accept,* and *agree to* are all equivalent. It is best to use the word *adopt.*

Forms of the Motion

"I move that we adopt the recommendation of the committee."

"I move that the auditor's report be adopted."

Rules Governing the Motion

1. Cannot interrupt a speaker

2. Requires recognition

3. Requires a second

4. Is debatable

5. Is amendable

6. Requires a majority vote

7. May be reconsidered

Amend

A subsidiary motion. This motion is made to change the wording of the motion before final action is taken on it.

There are two kinds of amendments, the primary (first degree) and the secondary (second degree) amendments. The primary amendment amends the pending motion and must be germane to it, that is, closely related to the motion. The secondary amendment amends the primary amendment and must be germane to it. Secondary amendments do not apply to the main motion. Only two amendments may be pending at one time. After they have been disposed of, another amendment may be made, if it is germane. When there are two amendments pending, the secondary amendment is voted on first, then the primary amendment. The main motion is then open for discussion before the final vote is taken.

Forms of the Motion

"I move to amend the motion by adding at the end . . . ."

"I move to amend the motion by striking out the word (or words) between . . . and . . . ."

"I move to insert the word (or words) between the word . . . and the word . . . ."

"I move to amend the motion by striking out the word (or words) and inserting the word (or words) between the word . . . and the word . . . ."

"I move to strike out the main motion and insert . . . ."

"I move to substitute the following . . . ."

Rules Governing the Motion

1. Is not in order when another has the floor

2. Requires recognition

3. Requires a second

4. Is debatable when applied to a debatable motion

5. Is amendable (a primary amendment is amendable; a secondary amendment is not)

6. Yields to higher ranking subsidiary motions and all privileged and applicable incidental motions, except motions to divide and to consider by paragraph or seriatim

7. Requires a majority vote even if the motion to be amended requires a higher vote (a primary amendment requires two votes, the first on the amendment and the second on the pending main motion; a secondary amendment requires three votes, the first on the secondary amendment, the second on the primary amendment, and the third on the pending main motion)

8. May be reconsidered

Amend Something Previously Adopted

A specific main motion. This is a motion by which an action previously adopted or taken can be changed, repealed, or annulled.

Forms of the Motion

"I move to amend the motion adopted at the January meeting by striking out . . . . Previous notice was given at the last meeting."

"I move to amend the motion relating to . . . adopted at the May meeting by inserting . . . . Previous notice has been given."

Rules Governing the Motion

1. Cannot interrupt a speaker

2. Requires recognition

3. Requires a second

4. Is debatable; debate may go into the merits of the motion which it is proposed to amend

5. Is amendable

6. Requires a two-thirds vote or a vote of a majority of the entire membership, except when notice has been given at a previous meeting; then the motion requires a majority vote

7. Only the negative vote may be reconsidered

Appeal

An incidental motion. This motion allows a member who disagrees with the ruling of the chair to have the assembly make the decision.

Form of the Motion

"I appeal from the decision of the chair."

Rules Governing the Motion

1. Is in order when another member has the floor; must be proposed immediately

2. Does not require recognition

3. Requires a second

4. Is debatable

5. Is not amendable

6. Requires a majority vote in the negative to overrule the chair's decision (a majority vote or tie vote sustains the decision of the chair)

7. Takes precedence over any question and must be decided immediately

Call for the Orders of the Day

A privileged motion. This motion requires that the assembly conform to its agenda, program, or order of business, or that it take up a general or special order due to come up.

When the orders of the day are called for, the chair may say, "Would the assembly care to finish this part of the business before adhering to the orders of the day?" If there is an affirmative vote, the business is completed before returning to the agenda.

Form of the Motion

"I call for the orders of the day."

Rules Governing the Motion

1. Is in order when another has the floor
2. Does not require recognition
3. Does not require a second
4. Is not debatable
5. Is not amendable
6. Upon the call by a single member, the chair must take up the prescribed order of business; no vote is necessary
7. Cannot be reconsidered

Close Debate

A subsidiary motion. This motion is to prevent or to stop discussion on the pending question or questions and to bring the pending question to an immediate vote.

Forms of the Motion

"I move to close debate on the motion."

"I move to close debate on all pending motions."

Rules Governing the Motion

1. Cannot interrupt a speaker

2. Requires recognition

3. Requires a second

4. Is not debatable

5. Is not amendable

6. Requires a two-thirds vote

7. Can be applied to debatable motions only

Close Nominations

An incidental motion. A nomination is a formal presentation of the member's name as a candidate for a particular office. When there are several candidates for an office, a member may wish to close nominations.

In cases when it appears that there are no further nominations for a particular office, the chair declares the nomination closed, or someone may move to close nominations. Usually no motion is necessary to close nominations, since they may be reopened by a motion to this effect.

Form of the Motion

"I move to close nominations."

Rules Governing the Motion

1. Cannot interrupt a speaker
2. Requires recognition
3. Requires a second
4. Is not debatable
5. Is amendable
6. Requires a two-thirds vote

Commit *or* Refer

A subsidiary motion. This motion is made to refer a pending motion to one or more persons. This motion may be applied to a main motion or to a main motion with adhering amendments.

Forms of the Motion

"I move to refer the question to a committee."

"I move to refer the motion to the . . . committee."

"I move to refer the motion to a committee of three appointed by the chair."

"I move to refer the question to the executive committee with power to act."

Rules Governing the Motion

1. Cannot interrupt a speaker

2. Requires recognition

3. Requires a second

4. Is debatable as to the desirability of committing and to the appropriate details of the motion to commit

5. Is amendable as to the committee composition, manner of composition, and instructions to the committee

6. Requires a majority vote

7. Can be reconsidered if the committee has not begun consideration of the question

Consider Informally

A subsidiary motion. This motion allows the members to speak informally on a motion. If this motion passes, the question is open to informal consideration. There is no limit to the number of times a member can speak on the question or on any amendment. As soon as the question has been voted upon, the informal consideration ceases.

Form of the Motion

"I move that we discuss this subject informally."

Rules Governing the Motion

1. Cannot interrupt a speaker
2. Requires recognition
3. Requires a second
4. Is debatable
5. Is not amendable
6. Requires a majority vote

Consider by Paragraph

An incidental motion. This motion provides for long motions or reports consisting of several paragraphs, resolutions, or sections to be considered by opening different parts to debate and amendment separately, without dividing the question.

Each paragraph is open to debate and amendment if the motion to consider by paragraph is adopted. When no further amendments are proposed and debate ceases on that paragraph, the chair proceeds to the next paragraph until all have been open to debate and amendment. After all paragraphs are amended, the entire series is open to further amendment and debate. At this time additional parts may be inserted or parts may be struck out. A single vote is then taken on the adoption of the entire series.

Forms of the Motion

"I move that the resolution be considered by paragraph."

"I move that the bylaws be considered by sections."

Rules Governing the Motion

1. Cannot interrupt a speaker
2. Requires recognition
3. Requires a second
4. Is not debatable
5. Is amendable
6. Requires a majority vote
7. Cannot be reconsidered

Discharge a Committee

A specific main motion. This is a motion by means of which further consideration of a subject may be taken away from a committee. The assembly can take the matter out of a committee's hands after it has been referred to it and before the committee has made a final report. So long as a question (subject) is in the hands of a committee, the assembly cannot consider another motion involving practically the same thing.

No motion is necessary to discharge a committee when the committee has given its final report to the assembly. The committee is then automatically discharged from further consideration of the matter.

Forms of the Motion

"I move that the committee to which was referred the motion regarding . . . be discharged."

"I move that the committee appointed to investigate the question of . . . be discharged and that this matter be made a special order of business at our next meeting."

"I move that the membership committee be discharged from further consideration of the motion referred to it on . . . ."

Rules Governing the Motion

1. Cannot interrupt a speaker

2. Requires recognition

3. Requires a second

4. Is debatable; debate may go into the merits of the question which is in the hands of the committee

5. Is amendable by the basic process of amending, and may instruct the committee instead of discharging it

6. Requires a two-thirds vote, or a vote of the majority of the entire membership, or only a majority vote if previous notice has been given at a previous meeting or in the call to the meeting

7. Only the negative vote may be reconsidered

Division of the Assembly

An incidental motion. This motion is used when a member doubts the result of a vote announced by the chair. A division must be called for before the chair states another motion. If a member wants the vote to be counted, he or she must make a motion to that effect.

Forms of the Motion

"I call for a division."

"Division."

Rules Governing the Motion

1. Can interrupt a speaker

2. Does not require recognition

3. Is not debatable

4. Is not amendable

5. Does not require a vote, since a single member can demand that a vote be taken by standing

Division of the Question

An incidental motion. The purpose of this motion is to divide a motion or an amendment if it consists of two or more parts, each part being capable of standing alone.

The motion must state clearly the manner in which the question is to be divided. A motion cannot be divided unless each part presents a proper question for the assembly to act on if none of the other parts is adopted. A resolution cannot be divided if it contains several parts which would be impossible to separate without rewriting the resolution.

Forms of the Motion

"I move to divide the motion so as to consider separately the . . . and the . . . ."

"I move to divide the resolution so as to consider separately the question on . . . and the question on . . . ."

Rules Governing the Motion

1. Cannot interrupt a speaker
2. Requires recognition
3. Requires a second
4. Is not debatable
5. Is amendable
6. Requires a majority vote
7. Cannot be reconsidered

Lay on the Table (Temporarily)

A subsidiary motion. This motion puts aside the pending question temporarily when something more urgent arises. The motion to lay on the table cannot be qualified in any way. The motion to use is to postpone to a certain time.

When the motion is laid on the table, all adhering motions go with it. When taken from the table, the motion comes back exactly as it was, with all the adhering motions.

The motion to lay on the table may be taken from the table on the same day, provided that some other business has taken place. If the motion is not taken from the table at the close of the next regular business meeting, the question dies. However, the matter can be taken up as new business at a later meeting.

Forms of the Motion

"I move to lay the question on the table."

"I move that the resolution be laid on the table."

Rules Governing the Motion

1. Cannot interrupt a speaker

2. Requires recognition

3. Requires a second

4. Is not debatable; however, a member may make a short statement as to the reason for making the motion

5. Is not amendable

6. Requires a majority vote

Limit or Extend Debate

A subsidiary motion. This motion is to limit the time that will be devoted to the discussion of a pending question, or to lengthen the time of discussion.

Forms of the Motion

"I move to limit debate on the motion to one hour."

"I move to limit the time of each speaker on the motion to three minutes."

"I move that the time of the speaker be extended by ten minutes."

Rules Governing the Motion

1. Cannot interrupt a speaker

2. Requires recognition

3. Is not debatable

4. Is amendable only as to time

5. Requires a two-thirds vote

6. Can be reconsidered

Main Motion

The main motion brings a subject before the assembly for its discussion and decision.

Motions that can be made while the main motion is pending include: all subsidiary and all privileged motions; and applicable incidental motions, such as: division of the question, consider by paragraph, withdraw, object to the consideration of an original main motion.

A main motion should be stated in the affirmative, since the negative form often confuses members in voting. Avoid saying, "I move that we do not increase our dues." The motion can be clearly stated by saying, "I move that our dues remain the same." A main motion should be concise, clear, and made as complete as possible so as to avoid amendments.

Forms of the Motion

"I move that we establish a scholarship fund."

"I move the adoption of the following resolution, RESOLVED: That . . . ."

Rules Governing the Motion

1. Cannot interrupt a speaker

2. Requires recognition

3. Requires a second

4. Is debatable

5. Is amendable

6. Yields to all subsidiary, privileged, or applicable incidental motions

7. Requires a majority vote, except when the bylaws require a greater vote; when adoption would have the effect of suspending a rule of order or a parliamentary right; or when adoption would have the effect of rescinding or amending something previously adopted

8. May be reconsidered

Method of Voting

An incidental motion. This motion is used when some form other than voice vote is desired.

Form of the Motion

"I move that when we vote, we vote by ballot."

Rules Governing the Motion

1. Cannot interrupt a speaker

2. Requires recognition

3. Requires a second

4. Is not debatable

5. Is amendable

6. Requires a majority vote

Object to the Consideration of a Question

An incidental motion. This motion is used to avoid a particular embarrassing or undesirable original main motion from being discussed. If an objection is sustained, the motion is not before the assembly.

Form of the Motion

"I object to the consideration of the motion (resolution)."

Rules Governing the Motion

1. Can interrupt proceedings; must be made before the chair states the motion and before any debate
2. Does not require a second
3. Is not debatable
4. Is not amendable
5. Requires two-thirds vote against consideration to sustain the objection

Parliamentary Inquiry

An incidental motion. The purpose of this motion is to enable a member to ask the chair a question of procedure in connection with the pending question or with a motion that the member wishes to bring before the assembly immediately. It is also used to ask for information on the effect of the pending question.

Form of the Motion

"I rise to a parliamentary inquiry."

Rules Governing the Motion

1. Can interrupt a speaker if it requires an immediate answer

2. Requires no second

3. Is not debatable

4. Is not amendable

5. Requires no vote

6. Can have no motion applied to it

Point of Order

An incidental motion. This motion is to call to the attention of the chair a violation of a rule when the chair neglects to call it.

A point of order must be raised immediately. It cannot be brought up later unless the error involved a violation of the bylaws. The motion interrupts business. The presiding officer either rules that the point of order is well taken and orders the mistake or omission to be corrected, or rules that the point of order is not well taken and resumes business at the point where it was interrupted.

Forms of the Motion

"I rise to a point of order."

"Point of order."

Rules Governing the Motion

1. Can interrupt a speaker

2. Does not require recognition

3. Does not require a second

4. Is not debatable

5. Is not amendable

6. Does not require a vote as the chair decides; if submitted to the assembly, a majority vote is required

7. May not be reconsidered

Postpone Definitely (to a Certain Time)

A subsidiary motion. This is a motion by which action on a pending question can be put off, within limits, to a definite day, meeting, or hour, or until a certain event.

There are limits on postponement. A question can be postponed only until the close of the next session. In a convention, a motion may not be postponed beyond the last meeting of the convention.

Forms of the Motion

"I move to postpone consideration of the motion until 3 P.M."

"I move to postpone the question until our next meeting."

"I move to postpone consideration of this question until our next meeting, and that it be made a special order for 1:30 P.M."

Rules Governing the Motion

1. Cannot interrupt a speaker

2. Requires recognition

3. Requires a second

4. Is debatable only as to the propriety and details of postponement

5. Is amendable only as to time to which the question is to be postponed

6. Requires a majority vote in its simple form; requires a two-thirds vote if made a special order

7. Can be reconsidered

Previous Question (Stop Debate)

A subsidiary motion. The motion "previous question" is often misunderstood. It is a motion to stop debate and take an immediate vote on the pending question. Members sometimes call out "Question" without obtaining the floor. This is discourteous and disorderly.

If the previous question is adopted, votes are taken immediately on the question specified. If lost, debate continues on the immediately pending question.

Forms of the Motion

"I move to vote immediately on the motion."

"I move to vote now on all pending questions."

"I move the previous question."

Rules Governing the Motion

1. Cannot interrupt a speaker

2. Requires recognition

3. Requires a second

4. Is not debatable

5. Is not amendable

6. Requires a two-thirds vote

Question of Privilege

A privileged motion. This motion enables a member to secure immediate decision and action by the presiding officer on a request that concerns the comfort, convenience, rights, or privileges of the assembly or of the member. It is also used to request permission to present a motion of urgent nature, even though business is pending.

Forms of the Motion

"I rise to a question of privilege of the assembly."

"I rise to a question of personal privilege."

Rules Governing the Motion

1. Can interrupt a speaker if it requires an immediate answer

2. Does not require recognition

3. Is not debatable

4. Is not amendable

5. Requires no vote

6. Chair rules; ruling is subject to appeal

7. May not be reconsidered

8. Can have no motion applied to it except the motion to withdraw

Ratify

A specific main motion. To ratify means to approve, confirm, validate, or make legal. The object of the motion is to approve or legalize an action taken in an emergency or when no quorum was present.

Forms of the Motion

"I move to ratify the action taken by the executive committee."

"I move that we ratify the action taken by...."

Action already taken cannot become legally valid until approved by the assembly. The assembly can ratify such actions of its officers, committees, and delegates as it would have the right to authorize in advance. It cannot make valid a voice vote election when the bylaws require elections by ballot, nor can it ratify anything done in violation of national, state, or local law.

Rules Governing the Motion

1. Cannot interrupt a speaker

2. Requires recognition

3. Requires a second

4. Is debatable

5. Is amendable

6. Requires a majority vote

7. Can be reconsidered

Recess

A privileged motion. Recess is a short intermission in the assembly's proceedings which does not close the meeting, and after which business will be resumed at exactly where it was interrupted.

When a motion to recess is made when no business is pending, it is a main motion. When a recess is provided for in the adopted program, the chair, without further action by the assembly, announces the fact and declares the assembly to be in recess when that time comes. If the chair fails to announce the recess at that time, a member may call for the orders of the day.

Forms of the Motion

"I move that we recess for ten minutes."

"I move to recess until 2:30 P.M."

Rules Governing the Motion

1. Cannot interrupt a speaker

2. Requires recognition

3. Requires a second

4. Is not debatable

5. Is amendable as to the length of time of the recess

6. Requires a majority vote

7. May be reconsidered

Reconsider

A specific main motion. The purpose of the motion to reconsider a vote taken on a motion is to bring that motion again before the assembly, as though no vote had been taken on it.

The motion to reconsider can be made only on the same day or the next calendar day after the original vote was taken.

Form of the Motion

"I move to reconsider the vote taken on the motion relating to . . . ."

Rules Governing the Motion

1. Cannot interrupt a speaker

2. Requires recognition

3. Requires a second

4. Is debatable

5. Is not amendable

6. Requires a majority vote

7. Cannot be reconsidered

Rescind

A specific main motion. The purpose of the motion is to repeal (cancel, void) a main motion passed at a previous meeting. The effect of the motion to rescind is to strike out an entire motion, resolution, rule, or paragraph that has been adopted at some previous meeting. However, there is some action which cannot be rescinded. When something has been done as a result of a vote on the motion, it is impossible to undo it.

Form of the Motion

"I move to rescind the motion passed at the May meeting concerning . . . ."

Rules Governing the Motion

1. Cannot interrupt a speaker
2. Requires recognition
3. Requires a second
4. Is debatable and opens the motion it proposes to rescind to debate
5. Cannot be amended
6. Requires a majority vote with previous notice

Suspend the Rules

An incidental motion. This motion is used when the assembly wishes to do something that cannot be done without violating its own rules, but which does not conflict with the constitution or bylaws, local, state, or national laws, or with the fundamental rules of parliamentary procedure.

Rules that may not be suspended include: rules contained in the bylaws, constitution, or charter, unless that particular document specifies for its own suspension; rules protecting absentees or basic rights of the individual members.

Rules that may be suspended include: rules of order (parliamentary procedure) by a two-thirds vote; standing rules (rules that do not relate to parliamentary procedure, such as hours for meetings to begin or end).

Forms of the Motion

"I move to suspend rule number five."

"I move to suspend the rule which interferes with . . . ."

"I move to suspend the rule in order to take up . . . ."

Rules Governing the Motion

1. Cannot interrupt a speaker

2. Requires recognition

3. Requires a second

4. Is not debatable

5. Is not amendable

6. Requires a two-thirds vote

7. Can have no motions applied to it except to withdraw

8. Must be decided immediately

Take from the Table

A specific main motion. This motion is used when it is desired to bring back for further consideration a motion that was laid on the table.

Forms of the Motion

"I move to take from the table the motion relating to . . . ."

Rules Governing the Motion

1. Cannot interrupt a speaker
2. Requires recognition
3. Requires a second
4. Is not debatable
5. Is not amendable
6. Requires a majority vote
7. Cannot be reconsidered

Withdraw a Motion

An incidental motion. This motion allows a member who proposed a motion to remove it from consideration by the assembly. The consent of the seconder is not necessary. A motion can be withdrawn if there is no objection, or with permission from the assembly, up to the moment the final vote is taken.

Forms of the Motion

"I withdraw my motion." (before the motion has been stated by the chair)

"I request permission to withdraw my motion." (after the motion has been stated and discussed)

Rules Governing the Motion

1. Cannot interrupt a speaker

2. Requires recognition

3. Requires no second, as it is a request

4. Is not debatable

5. Is not amendable

6. Requires no vote

7. Can apply to all motions

Index

rules governing motion for, 95

Voting rights
of members, 36–37
of president, 18–19
of presiding officer, 18–19

W
Withdrawal of motion, 107–8
forms of, 108
rules governing, 108

NTC COMMUNICATION BOOKS

Speech Communication
The Basics of Speech, *Galvin, Cooper, & Gordon*
    The Basics of Speech Workbook, *Galvin & Cooper*
Contemporary Speech, *HopKins & Whitaker*
Creative Speaking, *Buys et al.*
    Creative Speaking Series
Dynamics of Speech, *Myers & Herndon*
Getting Started in Public Speaking, *Prentice & Payne*
Listening by Doing, *Galvin*
Literature Alive! *Gamble & Gamble*
Person to Person, *Galvin & Book*
    Person to Person Workbook, *Galvin & Book*
Self-Awareness, *Ratliffe & Herman*
Speaking by Doing, *Buys, Sills, & Beck*

Business Communication
Business Communication Today! *Thomas & Fryar*
Effective Group Communication, *Ratliffe & Stech*
Handbook for Business Writing, *Baugh, Fryar, & Thomas*
Meetings, *Pohl*
Successful Business Speaking, *Fryar & Thomas*
Successful Business Writing, *Sitzmann*
Successful Interviewing, *Sitzmann & Garcia*
Successful Problem Solving, *Fryar & Thomas*
Working in Groups, *Ratliffe & Stech*

For a current catalog and information about our complete line
of language arts books, write:
National Textbook Company,
a division of NTC Publishing Group
4255 West Touhy Avenue
Lincolnwood (Chicago), Illinois 60646-1975 U.S.A.